CZECH REPUBLIC

...in Pictures

Prepared by
Geography Department

Lerner Publications Company
Minneapolis

Photo © Massimo Sciacca

In Prague, the capital of the Czech Republic, a factory worker pauses during her shift.

This book is an all-new edition in the Visual Geography Series. Previous editions were published by Sterling Publishing Company, New York City. The text, set in 10/12 Century Textbook, is fully revised and updated, and new photogaphs, maps, charts, and captions have been added.

LIBRARY OF CONGRESS CATALOGING-IN-PUBLICATION DATA

Czech Republic in pictures / prepared by Geography Department, Lerner Publications Company.
p. cm.—(Visual geography series)
Includes index.
ISBN 0-8225-1879-1 (lib. bdg.)
1. Czech Republic. 2. Czech Republic—Pictorial works.
I. Lerner Publications Company. Geography Dept.
II. Series: Visual geography series (Minneapolis, Minn.)
DB2011.C88 1995
943.7—dc20 94-37432
CIP
AC

International Standard Book Number: 0-8225-1879-1
Library of Congress Catalog Card Number: 94-37432

VISUAL GEOGRAPHY SERIES®

Publisher
Harry Jonas Lerner
Senior Editor
Mary M. Rodgers
Editors
Tom Streissguth
Colleen Sexton
Photo Researchers
Erica Ackerberg
Beth Johnson
Editorial/Photo Assistant
Marybeth Campbell
Consultants/Contributors
Alena Cicelova
Dana Hurtova
Frank Jossi
Anna Kozelova
Magdalena Kratochvilova
Jozef Medvecky
Stefan Zambo
Sandra K. Davis
Designer
Jim Simondet
Cartographer
Carol F. Barrett
Indexer
Sylvia Timian
Production Manager
Gary J. Hansen

Independent Picture Service

Czech skiers hit the slopes at a winter resort.

Acknowledgments

Title page photo © Buddy Mays/Travel Stock

Czech accents, which affect Czech pronunciation, have not been used in this book.

Elevation contours adapted from *The Times Atlas of the World,* seventh comprehensive edition (New York: Times Books, 1985).

1 2 3 4 5 6 - JR - 00 99 98 97 96 95

Photo © Massimo Sciacca

Citizens of Prague enjoy a moment of leisure at a *zahrada*, or garden. A densely populated city, Prague includes several parks and open spaces as well as busy streets and sidewalks.

Contents

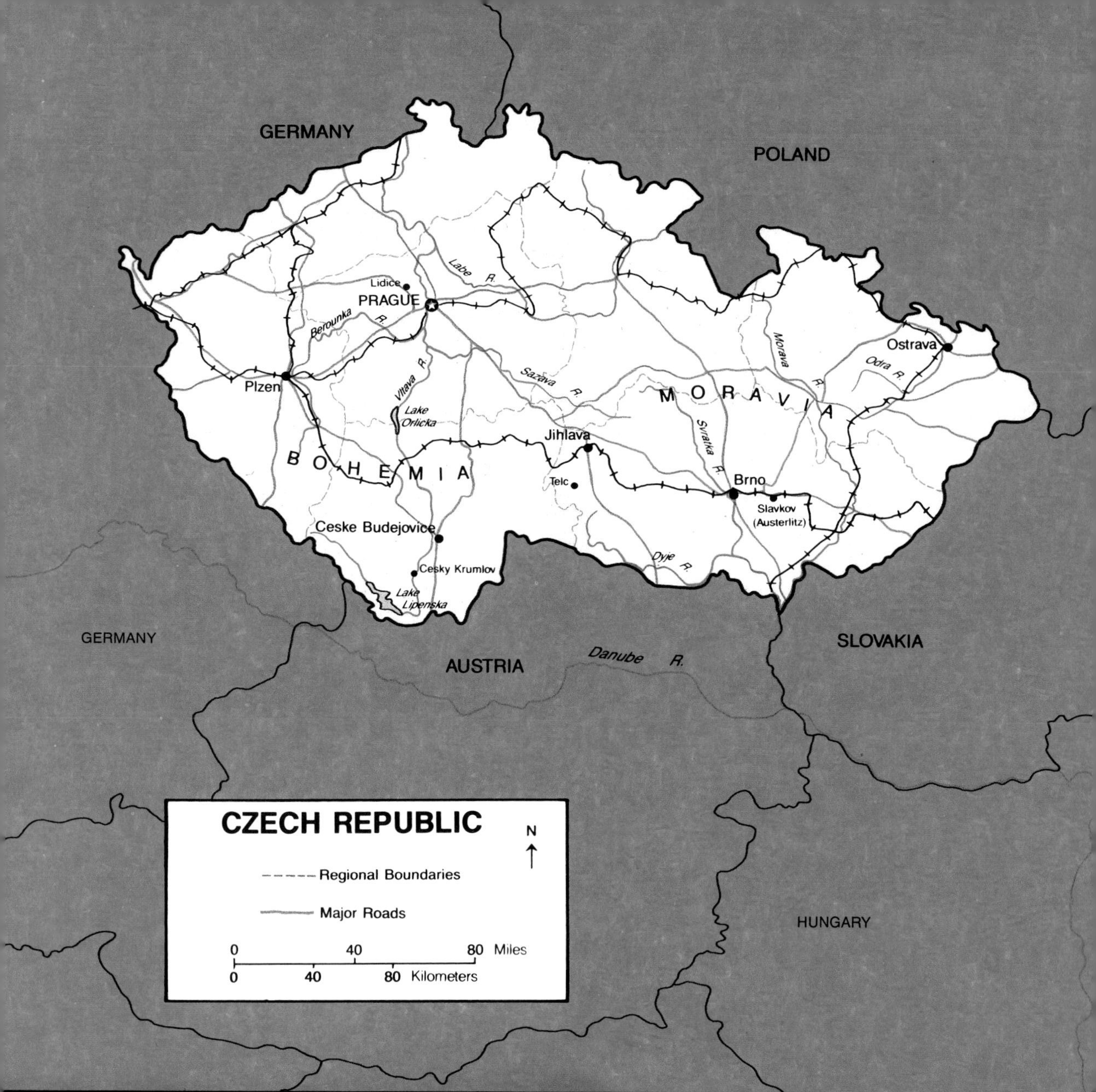

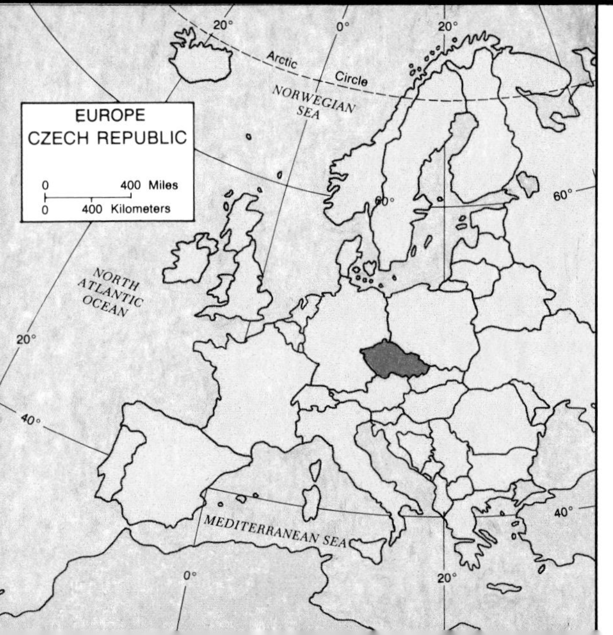

METRIC CONVERSION CHART
To Find Approximate Equivalents

WHEN YOU KNOW:	MULTIPLY BY:	TO FIND:
AREA		
acres	0.41	hectares
square miles	2.59	square kilometers
CAPACITY		
gallons	3.79	liters
LENGTH		
feet	30.48	centimeters
yards	0.91	meters
miles	1.61	kilometers
MASS (weight)		
pounds	0.45	kilograms
tons	0.91	metric tons
VOLUME		
cubic yards	0.77	cubic meters
TEMPERATURE		
degrees Fahrenheit	0.56 (*after* subtracting 32)	degrees Celsius

Photo © Massimo Sciacca

Workers replace cobblestones on an old street. Many Czech cities are undergoing renovation of their historic neighborhoods.

Introduction

Like many nations in central and eastern Europe, the Czech Republic has experienced several years of rapid change. A strict, one-party political system has been replaced by free elections and democracy. An economy closely controlled by the government is giving way to a free-market system, in which supply and demand determine wages and prices. Even the country is new—the Czech Republic was created in 1993 when Czechoslovakia split into two separate nations.

During the twentieth century, the Czechs have experienced wars, occupation by foreign powers, political instability, dictatorship, and economic decline. Yet the Czech Republic is also an impressive success story. It has long been an industrialized nation, and its people are known throughout Europe as hardworking and enterprising. Despite the recent political turmoil, many foreign companies have decided to invest in the country's growing economy.

Independent Picture Service

Karlstejn Castle rises on a wooded ridge in Bohemia, a region that makes up the western half of the Czech Republic. Designed in the fourteenth century, Karlstejn provided a retreat for the Bohemian king Charles IV. The top floors of the castle guarded holy relics and the Bohemian crown jewels, which were hidden in a safe with 19 locks.

Nevertheless, the Czech people are experiencing serious problems. The free-market system has forced unprofitable factories to close. Although unemployment is low, prices for basic goods and food are rising. In addition, industrial pollution is damaging the country's air, water, and soil.

The Czechs remain strongly united in their desire to overcome these problems and to adapt to a new economy. If they succeed, the Czech Republic could become a model for the many other struggling nations in central Europe.

Photo © Massimo Sciacca

The members of this band, like hundreds of other musicians, make a living by performing in the streets and public squares of the Czech capital.

The Sulovske Skaly are unusual sandstone rock formations that rise in the highlands of northern Bohemia.

Independent Picture Service

1) The Land

The Czech Republic is a small, landlocked nation in central Europe. The country has two major regions—Bohemia in the west and Moravia in the east. During the nation's long history, mountains and thick forests isolated these regions from surrounding countries. The Czech Republic's neighbors are Austria to the south, Germany to the west and north, Poland to the north, and Slovakia to the east. Slovakia and the Czech Republic together made up Czechoslovakia from 1918 until 1993, when the two nations split and became independent.

Covering 30,449 square miles, the Czech Republic is about the same size as the state of South Carolina. The greatest distance from north to south is 165 miles, and from west to east the Czech Republic stretches 300 miles.

Topography

Wooded hillsides, narrow valleys, and small, heavily farmed plateaus are common features of the Czech landscape. The Bohemian Basin, a plateau that covers much of northern Bohemia, is the country's most densely populated district. This productive area has fertile farmland as well as busy industrial districts. The Vltava River and several smaller waterways wind northward through Bohemia's narrow valleys. In southern Bohemia, small artificial lakes have formed behind dams that have been built along the rivers.

Mountains and uplands surround the Bohemian Basin. The Ore Mountains—known to Czechs as the Krusne Hory range—form a natural boundary in the northwest with Germany. The taller Krkonose (Giant) Mountains, also known as the Sudeten Mountains, border Poland in the northeast. This range includes Snezka (5,256 feet), the highest point in the Czech Republic.

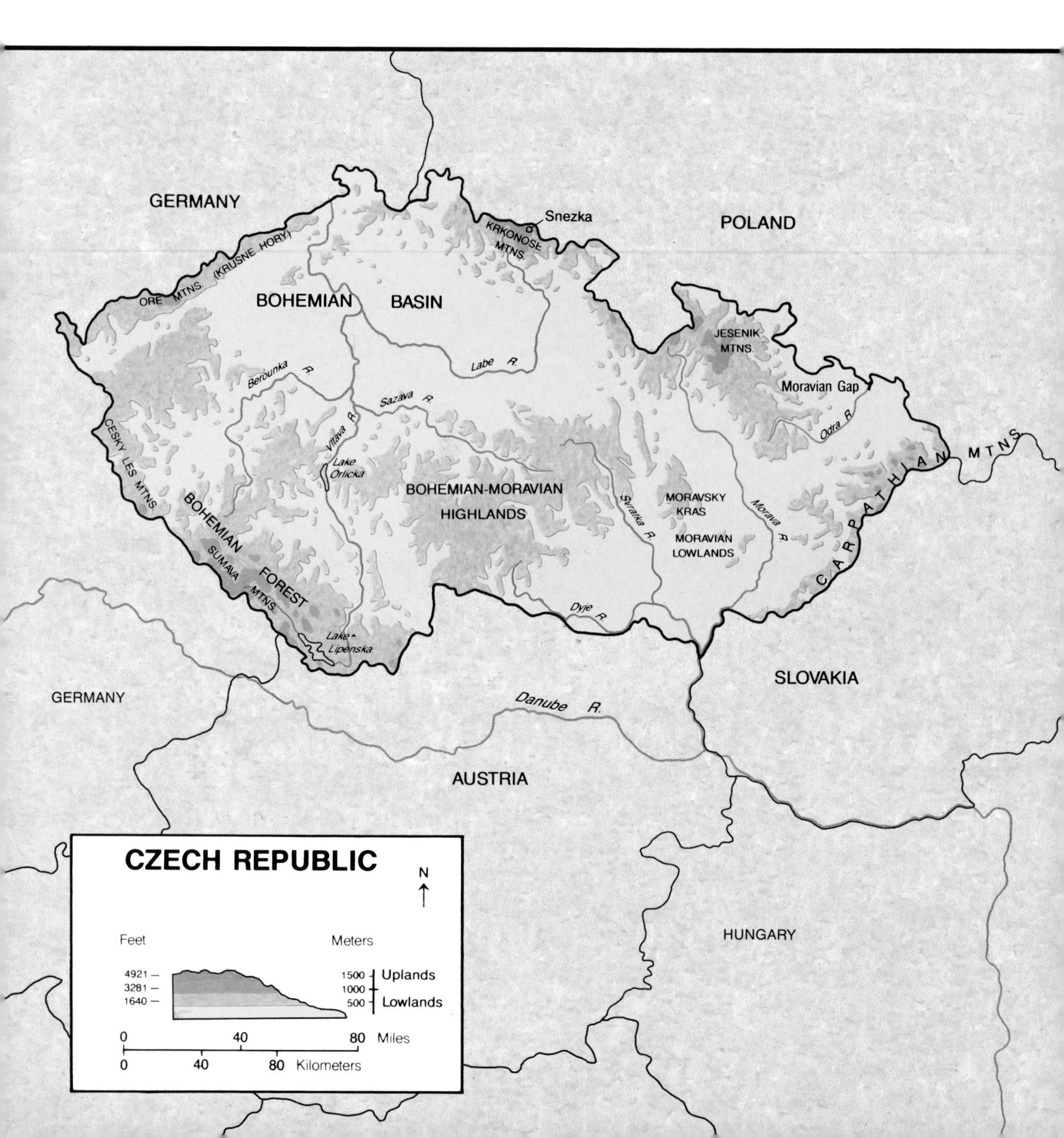

Photo by International Stock, Suzanne A. Vlamis

Hikers explore a fog-shrouded lake in Bohemia. Dams have created several artifical lakes and reservoirs along the swift and narrow rivers of the region.

In southwestern Bohemia are the Cesky Les and Sumava ranges, both of which have harsh climates, thick woodlands, and sparse populations. To the east of this region, which is also known as the Bohemian Forest, the Bohemian-Moravian Highlands stretch across the Czech Republic from central Bohemia into Moravia. Small towns and lakes dot the green hills of these highlands, which are crisscrossed by rivers and streams.

A mostly agricultural region, Moravia is divided in two by the Morava River. In the river's valley are industrial cities, mining centers, rural villages, and farms. West of the valley are the plains and low hills of the Moravian Lowlands. The Morava and other rivers of this area flow southward toward the Danube River, one of Europe's longest and busiest waterways.

The Jesenik Mountains rise in northern Moravia near the border with Poland. Rain and erosion have cut deep gorges through the soft sandstone hills of this range. South of the Jesenik Mountains is an area

Photo © Doug Plummer

A boy plays on the banks of the Vltava River. Swans, ducks, and other wildlife survive even where the river flows through busy urban environments.

of harder limestone rock known as the Moravsky Kras, where water erosion has formed caverns, underground streams, and strange rock formations. To the east lie the foothills of the Carpathian Mountains, which cross Slovakia.

Rivers

Sitting at a landlocked crossroads of central Europe, the Czech Republic has links to other nations along its principal waterways. Most of these rivers have not become busy shipping routes, however, because the Czech Republic lies far from the nearest ocean ports. Riverboats carry only about 5 percent of the nation's cargo, and most Czech goods still travel by road or rail.

The Labe River begins in the Krkonose Mountains and then flows southward into the fertile lands of the Bohemian Basin. The river curves to the west and north before entering a narrow valley in the Ore Mountains. After crossing the German border, the Labe becomes the Elbe and eventually reaches the North Sea, an arm of the Atlantic Ocean.

The Vltava River starts in a remote section of the Bohemian Forest. After leaving these highlands, the river turns sharply northward and cuts a narrow valley through southern Bohemia. Several smaller rivers, including the Sazava and Berounka, rush down from the surrounding highlands to join the Vltava.

The Vltava passes through Prague, the capital of the Czech Republic, before emptying into the Labe River. Barges and some passenger ships travel on the waterway. The Czech government plans to deepen the river's channel to improve it as a transportation route.

The Morava River flows from north to south through a densely populated valley in Moravia. The Odra, a mountain river in the north, traces a northward course into Poland. The Dyje and Svratka rivers join in southern Moravia and eventually reach the Morava, which in turn empties into the Danube.

Independent Picture Service

A narrow sidewalk crosses Bohemia's Pravcicka Brana, the largest rock arch in Europe.

Climate

The Czech Republic has a variable climate, in which altitude affects both temperature and precipitation. Summers are warm, with frequent thunderstorms. In Prague the average temperature in July, the warmest month, is 69° F. The plains of southern Moravia record the country's highest summertime temperatures.

Winters in the Czech Republic are long, cold, and usually dry. Many days are cloudy, with light snow and rain. Prague averages 31° F in January, the coldest month. Brno and other Moravian cities are usually colder. Snow covers the mountains of the Czech Republic from November to April, but people living in the lowlands rarely see heavy snowfalls.

Throughout the year, temperatures are cooler in the highland regions. Winds from the Atlantic Ocean to the west and the Adriatic Sea to the south bring more than 40 inches of annual rainfall to the mountains of Bohemia. But these ranges also block precipitation at lower elevations. As a result, the plains and valleys of the Czech Republic get less than 25 inches of rain and snow during an average year.

Independent Picture Service

A winter storm has blanketed this ski lift with snow and ice. Cold winds from the north bring snowfall to the mountains of the Czech Republic in winter.

Flora and Fauna

Dense forests, mainly in mountainous areas, cover about one-third of the Czech Republic. More than half of the nation's land has been cleared for farming and industry. Acid rain, which is rain tainted by pollution from heavy industries, has also destroyed large forests in Bohemia, especially in the Ore Mountains.

Coniferous (evergreen) trees, such as spruce and fir, thrive in the highlands at elevations above 2,500 feet. Beech trees are common in the hills of Bohemia and Moravia, and oak forests line the valleys of the Labe and Morava rivers. Many Czech lowlands have mixed forests of ash, maple, oak, and spruce trees. Wild grasses, clover, and reeds are common along the riverbanks.

Independent Picture Service

The forests of the Czech Republic abound in many varieties of wild game, such as these deer.

Photo by BTE Bilde

Dead and dying trees cover a Czech hillside. Coal-burning factories have polluted the air and have caused extensive damage to the country's forests.

Deer, foxes, boars, and chamois (antelope) live in the remote mountains and forests of the Czech Republic, which are also home to the moufflon, a mountain sheep. Hare and badgers inhabit the lowlands. Common birds include wild geese, partridges, pheasants, and wild ducks.

Natural Resources

Fertile soil, the country's most valuable natural resource, has allowed the Czechs to become self-sufficient in food production. The country's mineral resources include coal, a fuel source that is abundant in northern Moravia, in the valley of the Odra River, and near the city of Plzen in western Bohemia. The Ore Mountains have large deposits of lignite, or brown coal, which is burned to generate electricity.

Workers in the Czech Republic also mine mercury, lead, and zinc. Iron ore and magnesite provide raw materials needed by the steel industry. Supplies of uranium ore fuel the nation's nuclear power plants. The largest deposits of these minerals are found in the Ore Mountains. But the stock of metal ores is steadily dwindling, and little new exploration is under way to discover new supplies.

Although the Czech Republic has fields of oil and natural gas, the reserves are too small to meet the growing demand for gasoline and for fuel to heat homes. The rapids of the Vltava River power several hydroelectric plants, which convert the energy of flowing water into electricity.

Cities

During the nineteenth century, industrialization and the spread of railroads helped the country's cities to grow rapidly. About half the nation's 10.3 million citizens now live in urban areas of more than 20,000 people. The largest cities, such as Prague

The Old Town Hall is one of Prague's best-known historic landmarks.

Photo © Don Eastman

and Brno, are located near major rivers. The mountainous regions of both Bohemia and Moravia are home to small towns and villages.

PRAGUE

A bustling city of 1.2 million, Prague (called Praha in the Czech language) lies along the hills and bluffs of the Vltava River Valley in north central Bohemia. The historic capital of Bohemia, Prague is now the economic and political center of the Czech Republic, as well as an important cultural hub of central Europe.

A trading post on the site of modern Prague existed at least 2,000 years ago. After the city's founding in the ninth century A.D., Prague became the seat of Bohemia's kings. In the 1300s, Charles IV

Photo © Don Eastman

Prague's Nerudova Street has kept the same appearance for centuries. Nerudova Street and the rest of the capital survived the world wars of the twentieth century without the fighting and bombing that damaged many other European cities.

After World War II (1939–1945), many Czechs moved to the cities from the countryside. To meet the demand for new housing, developers put up high-rise apartment buildings in the outskirts and suburbs of the cities.

Independent Picture Service

built new palaces, churches, bridges, and a neighborhood known as Nove Mesto (meaning "new town" in the Czech language). In 1883 Prague began extending its city limits to include several nearby towns. This greatly increased the city's population and land area. In 1918 Prague became the capital of the new Republic of Czechoslovakia.

Despite the two world wars fought in Europe during the twentieth century, Prague escaped aerial bombing and heavy damage. Much of the historic center, including Nove Mesto and Stare Mesto (Old Town), has survived. Prague Castle looms over the city from an imposing hill. The castle has an impressive art collection and also serves as the residence for the Czech president.

Important industries in Prague include banking, financial services, media, education, manufacturing, and tourism. Although Prague has long been the country's political and financial center, most heavy manufacturing plants are located in other Czech cities.

SECONDARY CITIES

Brno, the Czech Republic's second largest city, has a population of 393,000. Located in southern Moravia, Brno is an industrial hub that produces motorcycles,

Independent Picture Service

A bustling international trade fair takes place each year in Brno. A longtime center of industry and trade, Brno is the capital and largest city of Moravia, which makes up the eastern half of the Czech Republic.

textiles, and heavy machinery. Founded 1,000 years ago, it served as the capital of Moravia when the region was part of the Habsburg Empire. One of Brno's major attractions, Spilbrk Castle, was the site of a notorious prison under Habsburg control.

The Czech Republic's third largest city, Ostrava (population 325,000), lies near the Moravian Gap, a mountain pass that links Poland and Moravia. Many of Ostrava's citizens are of Polish descent, and the city has close cultural and economic ties to Poland. Factories in Ostrava produce iron and steel, machinery, and chemicals. These businesses employ thousands of workers, but they have also caused severe air pollution. As a result, Ostrava is one of the unhealthiest urban centers in the Czech Republic.

Plzen (population 175,000), a city in western Bohemia, dates to the tenth century A.D. Although most famous for its Pilsner beer, Plzen has also been a center of weapons production. The huge Skoda factory, for example, once made armaments as well as aircraft, heavy machinery, railroad cars, and textiles. The city also has an important college of engineering that prepares its students for careers in industry.

Independent Picture Service

A church spire towers above the historic city of Plzen. Plzen was founded in western Bohemia around the tenth century A.D. and has since become a famous beermaking center.

Photo by Lenka Bradikova

Pernstejn Castle near Brno is one of many historic fortresses that dot the countryside of the Czech Republic.

2) History and Government

What is now the Czech Republic has been inhabited since prehistoric times, when cave dwellers lived in the region's mountains and valleys. About 500 B.C., groups of nomadic Celts arrived from northern and eastern Europe. The Boii, a Celtic people, settled in Bohemia and gave the region its name. Their villages and their largest city, Boiohemum, prospered from trade. But the Boii also fought with the Teutons, a people who had settled in lands to the west. By 12 B.C., a Teutonic group known as the Marcomanni had conquered the territory of the Boii.

For several centuries, Bohemia and Moravia were turbulent regions where nomadic invaders clashed over land and trade. Other Teutonic peoples defeated the Marcomanni and settled in the valleys of the south, while Avars and Slavs arrived from the east. Soldiers of the Roman Empire marched through the Bohemian Forest to build outposts in the Vltava River Valley.

By the third century A.D., the Romans had built a huge empire from their base on the Italian Peninsula in southern Europe. But foreign invasions and political conflict weakened the empire, which split into western and eastern halves in the fourth century A.D. This division later had a great impact on the peoples of central Europe.

After the split, Constantinople (modern Istanbul, Turkey) became the capital of the Eastern Roman, or Byzantine, Empire. Rome continued as the principal city of the Western Roman Empire. Both of these cities remained important centers of Christianity, a Middle Eastern faith that the Roman Empire had adopted as its official religion.

In the A.D. 400s, Teutonic groups pushed into southern Europe and Italy, and the Western Roman Empire collapsed. After the Teutonic invasions, huge numbers of Slavs began moving into central Europe. The largest group of Slavs to arrive in Bohemia during this "Great Migration" were the Cechove, or Czechs.

The Slavs had divided into eastern, southern, and western groups. The eastern Slavs settled in Russia, while the southern Slavs moved into the Balkan Peninsula of southeastern Europe. The western Slavs built their villages in the plains and river valleys of north central Europe. Ever since the Great Migration, western Slavs have made up the largest ethnic group in Poland, Bohemia, Moravia, and Slovakia.

Samo's Kingdom

In the sixth century A.D., the Slavs suffered a devastating invasion by the Avars, who came from central Asia. The Avars ruled Bohemia until a German merchant named Samo arrived in the early seventh century. Samo allied with the Czechs, defeated the Avars, and established a new state under his rule in 625.

Twelve years later, the kingdom defeated the Franks, who were attacking from their homeland in Germany. Bohemia remained independent until 658—the year of Samo's death. For more than 100 years afterwards, the Czechs fought Avars, Poles, and the Franks for control of the region. By 805 Bohemia and Moravia were paying tribute (money) to the Frankish ruler Charlemagne,

A worker digs in the ruins of an ancient hilltop fortification. After the Slavic migration of the sixth century, Bohemia and much of central Europe experienced nearly constant warfare as early settlers competed for land and resources.

Independent Picture Service

Photo © Erwin C. "Bud" Nielsen

In the late 700s, Charlemagne, the emperor of the Franks, united much of Europe under his rule and made Bohemia a march. This protective frontier region shielded the Frankish empire from invasions from the east.

who made these regions into frontier provinces of his realm.

A brilliant military leader, Charlemagne had destroyed the Avars and united much of western and northern Europe into the Frankish Empire. Closely allied with the Roman church, the Franks forcibly converted many Slavic groups to Christianity.

After Charlemagne's death in 814, the Frankish Empire was divided among his descendants. Ludwig, a grandson of Charlemagne, became the ruler of East Francia, which was made up of several powerful duchies (realms of dukes) in what is now Germany. These states would often interfere in the affairs of the Czechs in the coming centuries.

Photo by Lenka Bradikova

A castle ruin guards a plain in Moravia. The Great Moravian Empire was one of the strongest states of central Europe before invading Magyars destroyed it in the tenth century.

Missionaries and Magyars

In 830 a Slavic chief named Mojmir founded the Great Moravian Empire, a state that included parts of Bohemia, Moravia, Poland, and Slovakia. Under Mojmir and his successor, Rastislav, this realm remained under constant threat from the powerful German duchies.

To strengthen their realm, the rulers of Moravia formed closer ties to the Byzantine Empire. Although Mojmir and other Slavic leaders had accepted the Roman Catholic faith, Rastislav invited the Byzantine (eastern) church to send missionaries into Moravia. The Byzantine monks Cyril and Methodius, who arrived in 863, taught the Slavs Christian prayers and rituals in the Slavic language. To translate the Bible into this tongue, the missionaries also devised a new lettering system known as the Cyrillic alphabet.

Meanwhile, Rastislav was leading military campaigns in Germany. But in 870 his nephew, Svatopluk, captured him and surrendered him to the German king. Four years later, Svatopluk and this king signed a peace treaty, and Svatopluk turned his people to the Catholic church. While the southern and eastern Slavs stayed within the Byzantine church, the western Slavs—including Bohemians and Moravians—became loyal Roman Catholics.

After the death of Svatopluk in 894, the Magyars of central Asia invaded Europe. The powerful Magyar cavalry destroyed the Great Moravian Empire. After establishing the Kingdom of Hungary to the southeast, the Magyars began an occupation of what is now Slovakia that would last for nearly 1,000 years.

At the same time, the Premyslids—a group of Czech princes—had broken away from Moravia and were extending their rule over Bohemia. One of these leaders, Prince Wenceslas, swore allegiance to the German king Henry I in 929. This action roused the anger of Bohemia's princes, and Boleslav, the brother of Wenceslas, conspired to murder him in 935. Boleslav then became the second ruler of the Premyslid dynasty (family of rulers). During his reign, Bohemia took control of much of southern Poland.

The members of the Premyslid dynasty often quarreled among themselves over who would succeed to the throne. The turmoil allowed the wealthy nobles who controlled vast estates in the countryside to claim independence from the kings. Tiring of the conflicts, the people of Bohemia deposed the Premyslid king in the early eleventh century. They invited Vladislav, the ruler of Poland, to become their new leader.

Vladislav allied with the German king and brought Bohemia into the Holy Roman Empire. This huge state included hundreds of cities, kingdoms, and principalities (realms of princes) in central and eastern Europe. Bohemia became a fief—a state that paid tribute to the Holy Roman emperor.

Photo by Czech News Agency

In the ninth century, the Greek missionaries Cyril *(left)* and Methodius brought Christianity to the Slavs of the Great Moravian Empire. To translate the gospels into the Slavic language, they also created the new Cyrillic alphabet.

Return of the Premyslids

In 1037, after the death of Vladislav, the Premyslid dynasty regained the throne of Bohemia. To end the dynasty's conflicts, the Premyslid king Bretislav decreed that only the eldest member of his family could assume the throne. Bretislav also encouraged Germans to immigrate into the kingdom. By developing a stronger class of foreign merchants and artisans in the cities, the king and his successors hoped to weaken Bohemia's rebellious nobility in the countryside.

The German immigrants founded settlements throughout western and northern Bohemia. The kingdom adopted a German law code and carried on much of its trade with German cities. The Holy Roman emperors sent German clergy into Bohemia to strengthen German influence, which would remain an important factor in Bohemia's history.

Through military conquest and a marriage alliance, the Premyslid king Otakar II gained extensive lands in Austria, a principality to the south. But Otakar died in 1278 while fighting Rudolf II, an Austrian noble. After this battle, Rudolf founded the Habsburg dynasty, which would become the hereditary ruling house of the Holy Roman Empire.

The Premyslid dynasty came to a sudden end when Wenceslas III, who had no successor, died in 1306. John of Luxembourg, a foreign king who married a Premyslid princess, claimed the throne of Bohemia in 1310. Not all Bohemians accepted John as their monarch, however. For many years, the kingdom suffered civil war as the nobles fought with John and with one another for power.

The reign of John's successor, Charles IV, was known in Bohemia as the Golden Age. Charles strengthened the royal administration and added several fiefs to the kingdom. In 1355 he also became the Holy Roman emperor. During his reign, Charles IV issued a new law known as the Golden Bull. By this code, the Holy Roman emperor would be chosen by seven electors, one of whom would be the king of Bohemia. The Golden Bull made Bohemia one of the most powerful states in central Europe.

Photo by Mansell Collection

Walls, guard towers, fortifications, and churches rise along the banks of the Vltava River in this fifteenth-century illustration of Prague. The Karluv Most (Charles Bridge), built a century earlier, still crosses the river in the heart of the city.

Photo by Mansell Collection

A statue of Charles IV commemorates this brilliant ruler, who established a hereditary monarchy in Bohemia, founded the University of Prague, and was elected to rule the Holy Roman Empire in 1355.

Charles transformed Prague into an imperial capital by raising new buildings, churches, and monuments. He refurbished Prague Castle—the ancient seat of Bohemia's kings—and made the city into a center of learning by founding the University of Prague in 1348.

The Hussite Wars

In the mid-1300s, Bohemian religious leaders were beginning to question the power and vast wealth of the Catholic church and the popes who ruled it. Many of Bohemia's Catholic priests joined a movement for religious reform. Although many Czechs supported these priests, most Germans in Bohemia remained loyal to the pope.

After the death of Charles IV in 1378, religious clashes broke out between Czechs and Germans. Jan Hus, the rector (head) of the University of Prague, rebelled against the pope's authority. Hus quickly gained a wide following among the Czechs, who saw him as an important symbol of their independence from the Holy Roman Empire and from German authority. But in 1415, Catholic leaders captured Hus, who was condemned and burned at the stake.

The execution touched off decades of religious and ethnic warfare in Bohemia. German Catholics and Czech Hussites (supporters of Jan Hus) clashed in Prague and in many other cities. Jan Zizka, a Czech noble, led an army of Hussites that looted German towns and destroyed Catholic monasteries and churches. Zizka's

Independent Picture Service

Followers of Jan Hus march in a funeral procession for their executed leader. Hus's revolutionary religious ideas, and his execution by Roman Catholic officials, ignited a bloody revolt and a civil war in Bohemia that lasted twenty years.

Photo © Don Eastman

Since the establishment of the Roman Catholic Church in Bohemia, the archbishop's palace in Prague has been the church's local seat of power.

campaigns forced many ethnic Germans to flee Bohemia.

To retaliate, the pope called for a crusade (religious war) against Bohemia. Sigismund, the Catholic king of Hungary who had succeeded to the Bohemian throne, attacked Prague but was defeated by Zizka's forces. For several years, as the battles raged in Bohemia, the realm was without a king.

In 1458 the Bohemians elected George of Podebrady, a Hussite leader, as their king. But the pope and many Catholics opposed this ruler, who died without a successor in 1470. For years afterward, Czech nobles and townspeople formed rival camps and fought in support of their favorite candidates.

The Bohemian nobility took advantage of these conflicts to increase their power over the kingdom's townspeople and peasants. In 1487 the nobles established serfdom on their estates. Under this system, Czech peasants were bound to the estates as the legal property of the landowners.

Habsburgs Arrive

The religious and civil conflicts weakened Bohemia during a time of a serious foreign threat. In the early 1500s, an army of Ottoman Turks invaded central Europe from their base in Asia Minor (modern Turkey). Lajos, the king of both Hungary and Bohemia, died in battle against the Turks in 1526. To prevent Bohemia's conquest by the Ottoman army, the Czech parliament allied with the powerful Habsburgs of Austria and accepted a Habsburg prince, Ferdinand, as the new king.

Meanwhile, another religious rebellion was brewing in Wittenberg, Germany, where the priest Martin Luther was protesting corrupt practices of the Roman Catholic Church. When Luther began spreading his ideas to other cities, the Catholic church expelled him. Luther and his followers—known as Protestants—then founded an independent church. Both Czechs and Germans in Bohemia joined Luther's call for reform, and the Czechs founded a Protestant church in Bohemia.

Ferdinand and the Habsburg dynasty were loyal to the Catholic church and opposed to the Protestant Reformation. In 1547, after Ferdinand put down a rebellion by Czech Protestants, the Habsburg ruler declared Bohemia to be a Habsburg territory. Too weak to resist the Habsburg decree, Bohemia and Moravia would remain a part of the Habsburg Empire until the twentieth century.

Courtesy of Cultural and Tourism Office of the Turkish Embassy

An Ottoman army campaigns in central Europe during the sixteenth century.

Photo © Massimo Sciacca

The town of Telc suffered a devastating fire in 1530 that leveled all of its wooden homes. The townspeople soon rebuilt their dwellings in stone, with arcades (passageways) lining the main square.

Habsburg Rule and the Thirty Years' War

The Habsburgs controlled Bohemia—and the Holy Roman Empire—from their capital in Vienna, Austria. The wealthy estates and natural resources of Bohemia made the region one of the most important Habsburg possessions. Although German-speaking Catholics in Bohemia remained loyal to the Habsburgs, the Czech parliament—made up of the nobles, clergy, and townspeople of Bohemia and Moravia—opposed Habsburg rule.

The Habsburgs allowed Protestants freedom of worship, but conflict between Catholics and Protestants did not end. In 1617 Ferdinand II, a staunch ally of the Catholic church, inherited the Habsburg throne. Ferdinand was determined to stamp out Protestantism in the territories under his control. In 1618 a group of Czech nobles protested this policy by throwing three of Ferdinand's advisers out of a window at Prague Castle.

The advisers survived, but the Czechs were now in open rebellion. The parliament elected a Protestant to rule Bohemia and enlisted an army to fight the Habsburgs. In November 1620, the Habsburgs crushed the Czech forces at the Battle of White Mountain. After the battle, the Habsburg armies drove nearly all the rebellious Czech nobles out of Bohemia.

The defeat at White Mountain started the Thirty Years' War between the Catholic and Protestant states of Europe. Protestant armies from Germany, Denmark, and Sweden invaded Bohemia to battle the Habsburgs. The conflict caused widespread famine and destroyed Bohemian

Courtesy of Bildarchiv Preussischer Kulturbesitz

On May 23, 1618, angry Bohemian citizens threw three Habsburg ministers from a window in Prague Castle—an event known as the Defenestration of Prague. The citizens were protesting Habsburg rule over Bohemia. Fighting would soon break out between Bohemian Protestants and the armies of the Catholic Habsburgs, touching off the Thirty Years' War.

Glass factories were an important part of the industrial sector in eighteenth-century Bohemia. The many factories in the region made it the most productive state in the Habsburg Empire and one of the wealthiest areas of Europe. In modern times, workers continue to mass-produce decorative wares.

Photo by Czech News Agency

cities, towns, and farms. Ferdinand expelled nearly all Czech Protestants and stripped the Bohemian parliament of its power to make and enforce laws.

In 1648 the Treaty of Westphalia ended the war. By the terms of the treaty, Bohemia and Moravia remained Habsburg territories. Czech Protestants who had not died in battle were forced to leave the kingdom. In the years following the war, German Catholics seized the lands of Czech nobles and peasants. The Habsburgs prohibited teaching and publishing in the Czech language, and German became the official language of government and education.

Maria Theresa's Reign

After Maria Theresa became the Habsburg empress in 1740, she abolished the separate administration that the Habsburgs had used to govern Bohemia. This action drew Austria and Bohemia closer together and created a more efficient government. Under Maria Theresa's more liberal regime, Catholic control of education lessened and Czech culture began to revive.

Members of the Bohemian nobility started new industries, such as textile mills, glass factories, and coal mines. Bohemia, Austria, and Moravia formed a new customs union that helped trade among these regions and improved their economies. Bohemia soon became the most industrialized area of the entire Habsburg Empire.

Joseph II, who succeeded Maria Theresa in 1780, made further reforms in the Habsburg Empire. He granted complete freedom of worship to Protestants, wrote a new code of laws, and allowed the Czechs to publish a newspaper in the Czech language. Joseph also abolished serfdom throughout the realm. For the first time since the late fifteenth century, Czech peasants were free to leave their homes and farms. Bohemian and Moravian cities grew rapidly as new factory jobs attracted these farmers to the cities.

In the 1790s, a violent revolution in France led to the fall of the French monarchy. The leaders of the revolution pressed for a republican government, in which the power to pass laws would rest with an elected legislature. They also sought to abolish the wealth of the nobility and the power of the church. Rulers throughout Europe, including the Habsburgs, greatly feared the effect of this revolt on their own power.

Photo by Czech News Agency

Frantisek Palacky, a renowned historian, sought the creation of an autonomous Czech state that would include Bohemia, Moravia, and Silesia (an area that now covers southwestern Poland and southeastern Germany). But the Habsburg rulers of these regions opposed Palacky's ideas and defeated the Czech independence movement.

Within a few years, the French general Napoleon Bonaparte invaded Germany and Austria. Napoleon defeated the Habsburg forces at the Battle of Austerlitz in southern Moravia. This clash brought about the collapse of the Holy Roman Empire in 1806. The Habsburg ruler Francis II became the head of a new Austrian Empire, which included Austria, Bohemia, Moravia, Hungary, and parts of Poland and Italy.

National Revival

The French Revolution had inspired many European peoples to fight for republican government. By the 1840s, Czech writers and leaders were demanding political reform and an end to German influence in their nation. The historian Frantisek Palacky wrote the *History of the Czech People,* a book that revived interest in Czech history and culture. State schools began teaching the Czech language, and poets, novelists, and journalists used it in their works.

Palacky, who favored independence for Bohemia and Moravia, became a prominent Czech political leader. In June 1848, he was named head of the Slavic Congress, which met in Prague. The leaders of this congress pressed for more freedom for all the Slavic peoples—including Czechs, Poles, and Slovaks—who were living in the Austrian Empire.

Later that year, open revolt broke out in several European capitals, including Prague and Vienna. Despite the turmoil, the Habsburg ruler Franz Joseph rejected the changes proposed by the Slavic Congress. Habsburg forces put down the rebellion in Prague and installed strict martial rule over Bohemia and Moravia. In the 1860s, these regions became part of Austria-Hungary, a dual monarchy that replaced the old Austrian Empire.

Throughout the late 1800s, the longstanding conflict between Czechs and Germans in Bohemia worsened. While Czech nationalists attempted to win more freedom, German and Hungarian politicians in the Austrian parliament stopped the effort. The government, however, did begin writing laws for Bohemia and Moravia in the Czech language.

World War I and the Czechoslovak Republic

The Czechs were just one of many peoples to demand independence from Habsburg rule in the early twentieth century. The decline of the Ottoman Empire, which had ruled the Balkan Peninsula for centuries, also sparked revolt in southeastern Europe. As these challenges to Austrian and Turkish power grew, rival nations, including the Russian Empire, moved into central Europe to claim territory and influence.

These conflicts led to the outbreak of World War I (1914–1918). Austria fought the Serbs, one of the Slavic peoples seeking independence from Habsburg rule in the Balkans. In alliance with Germany, Austria also battled Russia in the east and Italy in the south.

The Czechs, however, had little desire to fight for Austria and Germany and against the Serbs and Russians, their fellow Slavs. Many Czechs fled to Russia to join a force made up of Czechs and Slovaks.

During the war, the Czech leaders Tomas Masaryk and Eduard Benes and the Slovak politician Milan Stefanik planned for an independent nation of Czechs and Slovaks. Masaryk promised the Slovaks a separate government within this postwar state. On October 18, 1918, as Germany and Austria suffered defeat on the battlefield, Masaryk declared the independence of a new Czechoslovak nation. Ten days later, Czechoslovakia was established, with Masaryk as its first president.

After the surrender of Germany and Austria in November 1918, the Habsburg monarchy collapsed. Austria and Hungary became separate nations, and the former Austrian territories in central Europe won their independence. At the same time, a violent revolution in Russia was leading to the founding of the Soviet Union, a

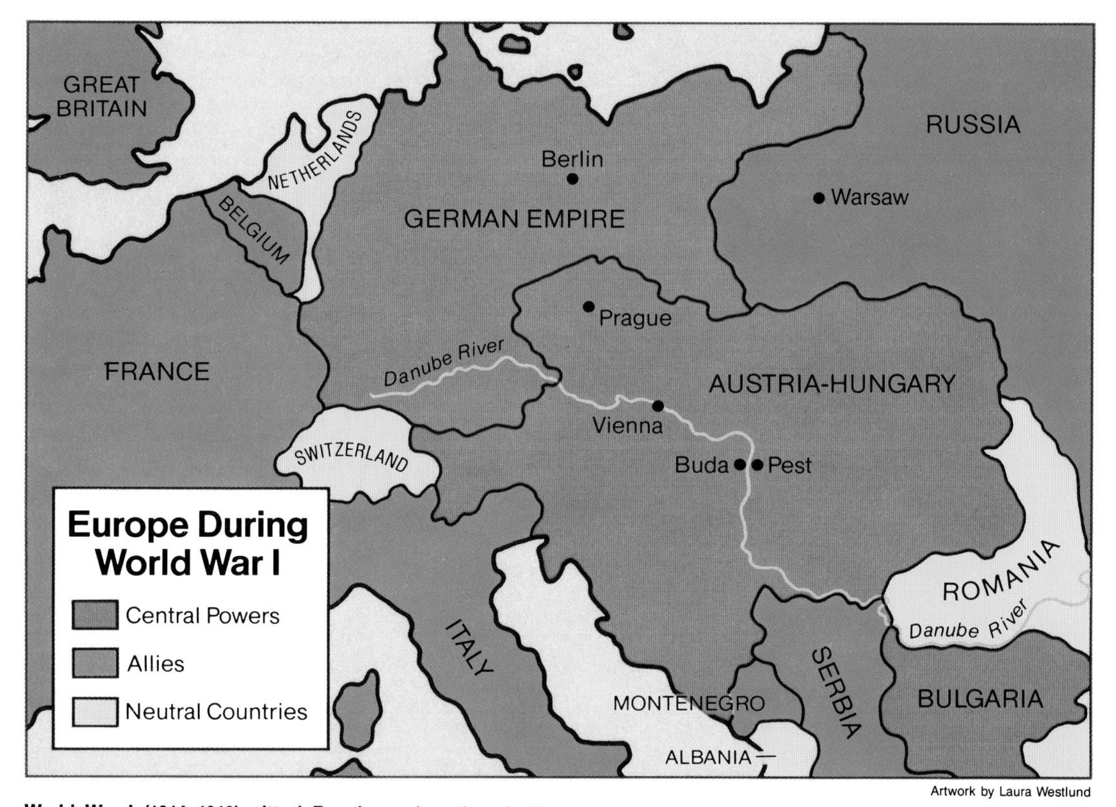

World War I (1914–1918) pitted Russia against Austria-Hungary. Although Bohemia and Moravia were still a part of Austria-Hungary, many Czech citizens deserted the Austrian army to fight alongside their fellow Slavs in Russia.

Tomas Masaryk led the new nation of Czechoslovakia—which included Bohemia, Moravia, and the eastern regions of Slovakia and Ruthenia—after its founding in 1918. A renowned writer, Masaryk also authored books on philosophy, politics, and history.

Photo by Archive Photos

Communist state that later controlled several eastern European nations.

The New Nation

The borders of Czechoslovakia included Bohemia, Moravia, Slovakia, and Ruthenia, a small region lying east of Slovakia. Several ethnic minorities lived within these borders, including Germans in the west and Hungarians in the southeast.

In 1920 the Czechoslovak legislature passed a constitution that established the bicameral (two-chamber) National Assembly. Despite Masaryk's promises to the Slovaks, no separate administration was created for Slovakia. Ethnic Czechs dominated the Czechoslovak legislature and judicial system.

Masaryk, who remained popular among Czech voters, won the presidential elections of 1920, 1927, and 1934. During this time, a coalition of Czech political parties shared power in the National Assembly. The Agrarian party represented farmers, while the National Democratic party was allied with industry and business leaders. The Communist party, which called for state ownership of farms and industries, remained a small faction of the Social Democratic party until 1921, when the Communists became independent.

Although the economy of Czechoslovakia benefited from new postwar industries, conflict among Czechoslovakia's many ethnic groups continued. Slovaks wanted self-rule, while Ruthenians and Hungarians felt little loyalty to the central government. Ethnic Germans, who made up about one-fourth of the total population, sought closer ties to Germany. (Because many Germans lived in the northern and western parts of Czechoslovakia—a region they called the Sudetenland—these people were also known as Sudeten Germans.)

Germans had little representation in the Czechoslovak legislature, however, and the nation's high taxes fell heaviest on wealthy German citizens. A program of land reform had allowed the government to seize German estates, which were then turned over to Czech peasants. The government also resettled ethnic Czechs in German-speaking regions. Although many Germans supported the government, others strongly opposed these measures and sought to unite the Sudetenland with Germany.

In the early 1930s, as a worldwide economic depression hurt German industries in Czechoslovakia, the nationalistic feelings of the ethnic Germans intensified. Sudeten German political parties won increasing popularity. After Adolf Hitler and the Nazi party took control of Germany in 1933, many Sudeten Germans allied themselves with Hitler, who threatened to annex (take over) the Sudetenland. Blaming Jews and Communists for Germany's economic and social problems, Hitler vowed to destroy his enemies and to establish an ethnic German empire in Europe.

Annexation and Occupation

After Germany annexed Austria in the spring of 1938, Britain, Italy, and France made a treaty with Hitler to avoid another world war. Called the Munich Agreement, the treaty allowed Germany to occupy all Czech territories in which more than half the population was German.

As a result, Germany received 38 percent of Czechoslovakia's land and now ruled 2.8 million Sudeten Germans and 750,000 Czechs. The German government also forced Eduard Benes—who had succeeded Masaryk as president in 1935—to resign. Emil Hacha, who accepted many German demands, then took the presidency.

Hitler still sought to occupy the rest of Czechoslovakia, whose weapons factories would help Germany's military. To avoid further conflict with Germany, Hacha's government agreed to grant independence to Slovakia and Ruthenia. Nevertheless, Hitler ordered an occupation of Bohemia and Moravia in March 1939. The small Czechoslovak army offered no resistance, and German troops quickly marched into Prague. Germany took control of Czechoslovak industries, and Bohemia and Moravia became a part of the Nazi empire.

Independent Picture Service

(From left to right) **Neville Chamberlain of Britain, Eduard Daladier of France, Adolf Hitler of Germany, and Benito Mussolini of Italy pose during their 1938 conference in Munich, Germany. Chamberlain and Daladier hoped to prevent war by allowing Hitler to annex (take over) part of Czechoslovakia. Although Germany soon occupied all of Czechoslovakia, Hitler and Mussolini launched World War II in September, 1939.**

Independent Picture Service

A crowd of Czechs presses forward as German troops enter Prague in March 1939.

WORLD WAR II

Germany's invasion of Poland in September 1939 touched off World War II. France, Britain, the United States, and the Soviet Union (the Allies) fought the Axis powers of Germany, Italy, and Japan. In Czechoslovakia millions of workers and students were forced to labor in factories to supply armaments for the German military. Opponents of the Nazis and nearly 100,000 Czech Jews were arrested and sent to concentration camps. Because Germany had already occupied most of Czechoslovakia, however, Czech cities suffered less fighting, bombing, and damage than other cities in central Europe.

Eduard Benes, who had fled to Britain, established a provisional Czechoslovak government in London during the war. Benes also signed a treaty of friendship with the Soviet Union. Meanwhile, Czechoslovak political parties formed guerrilla groups to fight against the Nazi occupation. The Czechoslovak Communist party, for example, organized a resistance movement from the Soviet capital of Moscow.

In the fall of 1944, the Czechoslovak guerrillas took advantage of German defeats in eastern Europe to step up fighting in Czechoslovakia. In May 1945, as Allied armies marched into the German

Independent Picture Service

In May 1942, Reinhard Heydrich, the German governor of Czechoslovakia, was assassinated while riding in an open car. The Germans responded by destroying the Czech village of Lidice, killing the village's male inhabitants, and sending the women and children of Lidice to concentration camps.

Photo by BTE Bilde

Factories spew smoke into the skies over Ostrava in Moravia. After World War II ended, Czechoslovakia's Communist government began a program of rapid industrialization that changed the landscape of many Czech cities.

capital of Berlin, a full-scale revolt broke out in Prague. When Germany surrendered on May 7, Soviet troops and Czechoslovak guerrillas took control of Prague, while U.S. armies occupied southern Bohemia.

After the war's end, the United States, Britain, and the Soviet Union met to decide the future of central Europe. The three nations agreed to revive the Czechoslovak state and to expel more than 2.5 million Sudeten Germans from the country. The new Czechoslovak government, under Eduard Benes, allied with the Soviet Union, which was extending its influence and control over many of Czechoslovakia's neighbors in central Europe.

Communism

The Czechoslovak Communist party won a majority of votes in the first postwar elections. For three years, the Communists shared power with other parties in a coalition government, with Benes serving as president. Klement Gottwald, the Communist prime minister, appointed several of his colleagues to head important ministries. Favoring state control of the economy, the Communists put many Czechoslovak industries under government ownership.

The growing power of the Communists alarmed many of their opponents in the government. In early 1948, several non-Communist ministers resigned to force new elections, which they believed the

Photo © Massimo Sciacca

New high-rise apartments housed the growing class of industrial workers after the war.

Independent Picture Service

Factory workers attend a Communist rally as Czechoslovak industries come under government ownership. The new government, following the example of the Communist regime in the Soviet Union, set wages and production quotas for all Czechoslovak industries.

Communists would lose. But instead of taking part in elections, the Communist party staged violent rallies in Prague. To avoid further turmoil, Benes appointed a new government dominated by Communist leaders.

In 1948 Gottwald replaced Benes as president. Gottwald's government banned opposition parties, turning Czechoslovakia into a strict one-party state. The media, schools, and the economy came under state control. Czechoslovakia—which was now made up of the Czech Socialist Republic and the Slovak Socialist Republic—drew closer to the Soviet Union. The nation also joined the Warsaw Pact, a military alliance of Europe's Communist nations.

Following the Soviet model, Czechoslovakia's government took over manufacturing, banking, and agriculture. The regime set high production goals and also fixed prices as well as workers' wages. The nation imported energy fuels from the Soviet Union, which also provided a market for Czechoslovak goods. Under the new system, most laborers worked long hours for low pay.

In the countryside, farmers were forced to pool their land and machinery and to join cooperatives, which could sell their crops and livestock only to the government at fixed prices. Land seized directly by the regime became part of a system of state farms, on which the farmers worked for wages. But, with little reward for increasing their harvests, Czech and Slovak farmers often failed to meet their production quotas.

Reform and Invasion

In the early 1960s, Czechoslovakia's economy began a sharp decline. The government invested little in modernization, and factories grew obsolete. State farms and cooperatives did not increase their harvests, and food shortages occurred. As the country's living standards worsened, some Czech and Slovak officials called for a change in the nation's political and economic systems.

In response, President Antonin Novotny gave some businesses more freedom to set their own wages and prices. But Novotny's government refused to abandon the system of central planning, to relax control of the media, or to legalize opposing political parties. In the mid-1960s, as the economy worsened, the president came under heavy criticism from within the Communist party.

Alexander Dubcek, the leader of the Slovak Communist party, challenged Novotny to quicken the pace of reform and to grant more independence to Slovakia. Dubcek carried the reform movement a step further by allowing freedom of the press in Slovakia. In January 1968, after winning support from other party members, Dubcek became the general secretary (leader) of the Czechoslovak Communist party. Two months later, Novotny resigned the presidency and was replaced by Ludvik Svoboda.

Under Dubcek's direction, the party lifted censorship and guaranteed freedom of religion and of the press throughout the country. Government controls over industries and farms eased, and the party promised increased independence for Slovakia.

These actions greatly alarmed Soviet officials and other Warsaw Pact leaders, who saw the reform of Communism as a threat to their own regimes. On August 20, 1968, several Warsaw Pact nations invaded

Photo by Archive Photos/Archive France

Civilians jeer at a passing tank during the invasion of Czechoslovakia by the Soviet Union and its allies in August 1968. Although street fighting broke out, demonstrators in Prague and in other cities were no match for Soviet tanks.

and occupied Czechoslovakia. Soviet officials then ordered the arrest of Dubcek, who was exiled from the country for a short time.

During the next two years, the party abandoned Dubcek's reforms, reimposed censorship, and again took control of the economy. Separate Czech and Slovak republics were founded within a federation. The Soviet Union stationed armed forces in Czechoslovakia, and Gustav Husak—a close ally of the Soviet leadership—replaced Dubcek as the Czechoslovak general secretary.

The Husak Regime

In 1975 Husak replaced Ludvik Svoboda as Czechoslovakia's president. While occupying the two most powerful positions in the Czechoslovak government, Husak became one of the Soviet Union's closest allies in central Europe.

At the same time, however, an organization emerged to fight for greater freedoms within Czechoslovakia. Called Charter 77, the group wrote a declaration protesting the harsh policies of the Husak regime. The leader of Charter 77 was Vaclav Havel, a playwright who criticized the government in many of his works.

Husak responded by imprisoning people who signed the document, including Havel, or by forcing them out of their jobs. Those caught publishing or reading the works of Husak's opponents were also punished. Despite these actions, illegal underground writings became widely popular among Czech and Slovak students and workers.

Although Czechoslovakia remained a strict Communist state, reforms were changing the Soviet Union. Mikhail Gorba-

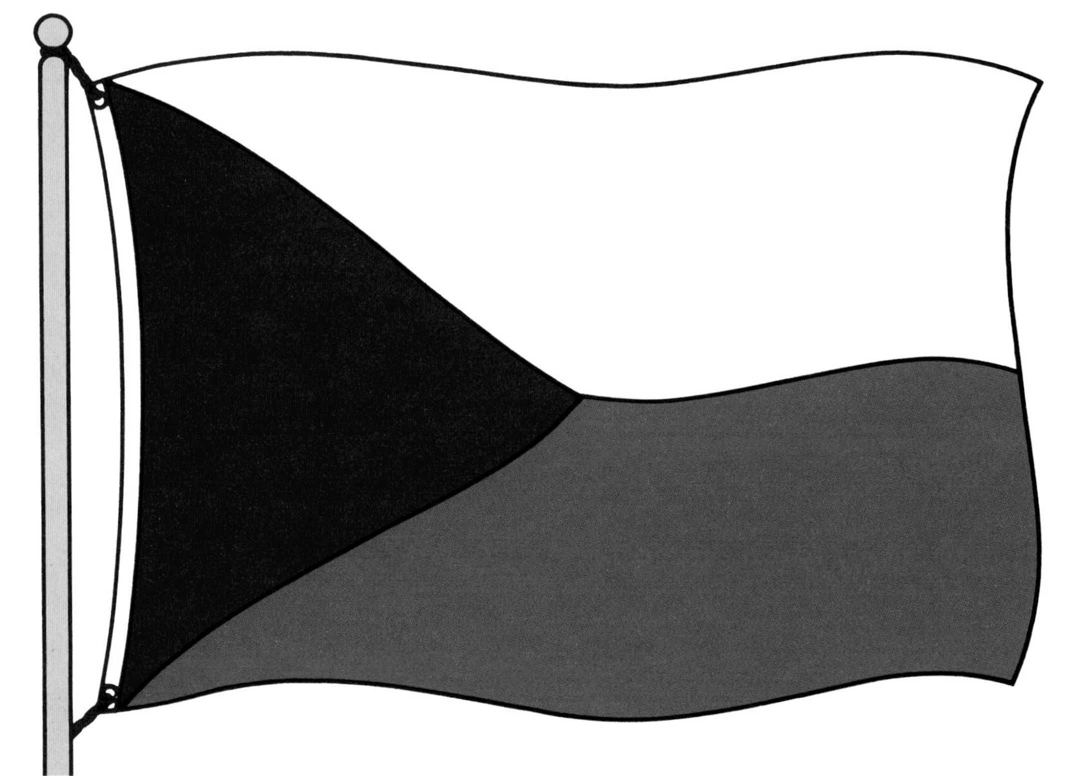

Artwork by Laura Westlund

Czechoslovakia adopted its flag soon after winning independence from Habsburg rule in 1918. Red and white are the colors of the Bohemian coat of arms, while blue is a traditional color of Slovakia.

Passersby examine campaign posters and literature during recent elections in the Czech Republic. Several new political parties and groups are competing for seats in the Czech legislature.

Photo by Bryan Ney

chev, who became the Soviet leader in 1985, eased restrictions on the media and allowed some privately owned businesses to operate. As a result, people throughout the Warsaw Pact demanded similar changes in their own countries. Husak, who refused to imitate Gorbachev's reforms, resigned as general secretary in 1987, although he remained Czechoslovakia's president.

Recent Events

In November 1989, several thousand opponents of the regime marched in Prague. A police attack on the demonstrators caused angry protests throughout the country. Under pressure to avoid further violence, Husak named a new cabinet with a majority of non-Communist members. Civic Forum, an opposition movement, was formed to field non-Communist candidates for office.

In the next month, a rally of 500,000 people and a general strike prompted Husak to resign. The legislature named Vaclav Havel as Husak's successor, and in June 1990 free elections took place. Civic Forum and Public Against Violence—a Slovak opposition party—defeated the Communists and took power in the Czechoslovak legislature.

Although the old regime was overthrown, the problem of reforming the

Photo by BTE Bilde

Prodemocracy marches in the fall of 1989—such as this one in Prague—brought about the fall of Czechoslovakia's Communist regime.

economy caused conflict in the new government. Some ministers favored the rapid transfer of state-run businesses to private owners, a process known as privatization. But Vladimir Meciar, a Slovak politician, sought a slower transition for Slovakia. Meciar claimed that privatization would greatly increase unemployment and poverty in Slovakia.

The new Czech leaders also argued for a strong central administration, with the government setting economic and foreign policy for Bohemia, Moravia, and Slovakia. But Meciar and other Slovak politicians wanted more independence from the Prague government. Czech and Slovak legislators

Photo by BTE Bilde

Alexander Dubcek, whose economic and social reforms triggered the Soviet-led invasion in August 1968, appears before the parliament of Czechoslovakia in 1990.

found themselves unable to reach an agreement on the nation's future constitution.

Elections in June 1992 made Meciar's party—Movement for a Democratic Slovakia—the second largest party in the legislature and the most powerful party in Slovakia. Meciar then formed an independent Slovak government with himself as prime minister. In November the legislature of Czechoslovakia agreed to disband the federation, and in January 1993 Slovakia became fully independent. The regions of Bohemia and Moravia made up the new Czech Republic.

Czech leaders have moved rapidly to privatize industries and to modernize the nation's banking system. The Czech Republic is also receiving money from international agencies to develop a free-market economy. The government has joined the United Nations and has applied for membership in the European Union (EU), an economic alliance of European nations. The Czechs are also forming partnerships with their neighbors in central Europe, including Hungary and Poland. By these actions, the government hopes to increase investment and production and eventually to provide a better standard of living for its people.

Government

The Czech parliament formally adopted a new constitution in December 1992. By its provisions, the Czech legislature consists of the Chamber of Deputies, whose 200 members serve four-year terms, and the Senate, whose 81 members sit for six-year terms. Legislators have the power to enact laws, to approve a national budget, and to pass international treaties signed by the president. Adults older than 18 years of age have the right to vote in legislative elections.

Both houses of the legislature elect the nation's president, who serves a five-year term. The president appoints the prime minister as well as the 18 members of the Council of Ministers. The president has the power to dissolve the legislature, to dismiss the prime minister, or to declare war. The president may not serve more than two consecutive terms.

The judicial system consists of a supreme court, a constitutional court, an administrative court, and regional and district courts. The president names the 15 judges of the constitutional court to 10-year terms. The constitutional court decides on legal matters of national importance.

The Czech Republic is divided into eight regions—six in Bohemia, and two in Moravia. The city of Prague forms one of these regions. Each of the regions, except for the capital, is further divided into several municipalities.

Courtesy of Embassy of the Czech Republic

Vaclav Havel spent time in prison for writing anti-Communist plays. After the Communist regime fell, the National Assembly elected him president.

Photo by International Stock, Michael Lichter

A crowd gathers after the polls close in June 1990. These were the first free elections held in Czechoslovakia since World War II.

3) The People

Ethnic Czechs—Bohemians and Moravians—are descended from ancient Slavic groups that invaded central Europe in the fifth century A.D. The Slavic Czechs migrated into the valleys and lowlands of Bohemia and Moravia, where many other ethnic groups—including Poles, Hungarians, Germans, and Slovaks—later settled. But the treaties that ended the world wars of the twentieth century forced many non-Czechs to move out of the country. Most Sudeten Germans, for example, were exiled to Germany after the end of World War II.

Bohemians form 81 percent of the population of 10.3 million, and Moravians account for 13 percent. Ethnic Slovaks—about 3 percent of the population—make up the nation's largest minority group. About 2 percent of the total population claim German or Polish ancestry. The Czech Republic also has a small population of Gypsies, a nomadic people who may have originally come to Europe from India.

Thousands of rural Czech families moved into cities after the end of World War II, and three-fourths of the Czech Republic's people now live in urban areas. The country's population density averages about 338 persons per square mile. Central Moravia and the industrialized regions of central and northern Bohemia have the highest densities. Mountainous areas have fewer cities and a much more scattered population.

Religion

The Czechs have been largely Roman Catholic since the 1100s. More than 60 percent of the republic's citizens are Catholics, although there has been a large minority of Czech Protestants ever since the Reformation of the the 1500s. The Reformed Church and the Czech Brethren are two important Protestant churches. Other Christian churches include the Old Catholic Church, the Czech Reformed Catholic Church, the Hussite Church, and the Uniate (Greek Catholic) Church. Prague once included a large Jewish population, but most Czech Jews were murdered in Nazi prison camps during World War II.

The Communist government saw religion as a dangerous rival for the loyalty of Czech citizens. To combat the influence of Protestant and Catholic sects, the regime took direct control of all religious organizations. The state chose who would lead the church and censored religious sermons. Catholic priests could not discuss child abuse and other topics that the government chose to ban. Many Czechs stopped attending services, and the nation's churches fell into disrepair or were closed.

After the fall of the Communist government in 1989, Czech churches opened their doors to worshipers again. Priests who had performed their duties in secret emerged from hiding. The Catholic church has gained new followers, and missionaries from other countries have arrived to win

The spires of the massive Cathedral of St. Vitus rise 400 feet above the streets of Prague. Begun in 1344, the church—the largest in the Czech Republic—was not completed until 1929. It has served as a coronation site, as a mausoleum (burial chamber) for Bohemia's kings, and as a place of religious pilgrimage.

Photo © Don Eastman

Students learn printing skills in a Czech public school, where classes are held in both academic and vocational subjects.

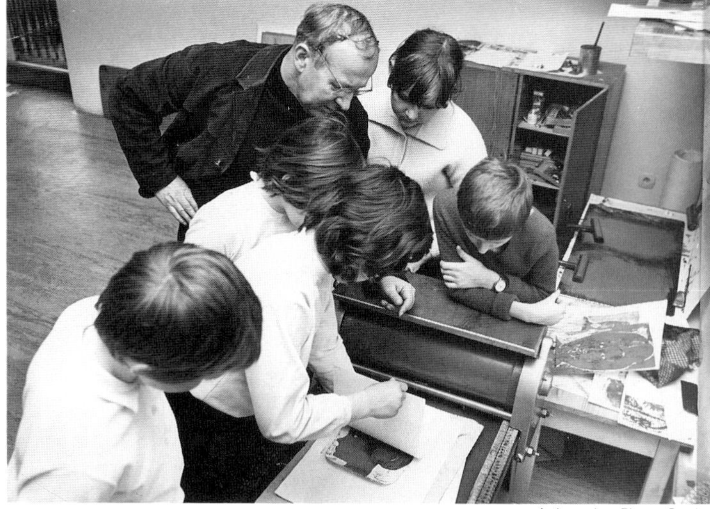

Independent Picture Service

converts to other Christian sects. In addition, crews are busy in Prague and other cities restoring historic churches and cathedrals.

Education and Health

Education has long been an important part of Czech life. The oldest university in central Europe is Charles University in Prague, which dates to 1348. Czech children were first required to attend school in 1869, and the nation has enjoyed nearly 100 percent literacy since the early 1900s.

In the past, Czech education was influenced by the country's rulers and political systems. The Habsburgs forced Czech students, teachers, and textbook authors to

Photo © Massimo Sciacca

Young Gypsies play on the streets of Jihlava, a city in the Bohemian-Moravian Highlands. Many Gypsies live in the outskirts of many Czech towns and isolate themselves from Czech society. As a result, they suffer high unemployment and poverty.

use the German language. Under Communism, teachers trained their students in socialist philosophy, which glorified farmers and laborers and criticized the wealthy. Religious and private schools were outlawed, while the government encouraged students from working-class families to attend public universities. Many upper-class students were denied postsecondary education.

In the 1990s, the new Czech government legalized private and religious schools and removed political teaching from the classroom. The nation now emphasizes science instruction and has made more money and resources available to all levels of the school system.

After three years of preschool, or *materska skola,* Czech students attend a *zakladni skola,* or basic school between the ages of 6 and 15. They may then enter a vocational school or a four-year school that prepares them for university studies. The nation has 23 universities or university-level institutions.

After World War II, the health-care system in Czechoslovakia was placed under state control. Doctors and nurses became state employees, and the government made free health care and medicine available to citizens. Health standards rose during the 1960s, especially in rural communities. But as the economy stalled, the state stopped buying new medical equipment for clinics and hospitals, and health-care standards declined.

In the early 1990s, the new government began privatizing hospitals and clinics and legalized private medical insurance companies. Health costs have risen, but the nation also has one of the world's highest ratios of doctors and hospital beds to population—an important measure of health standards.

Photo © Massimo Sciacca

Women rest in the main square of a small Czech town.

Average life expectancy in the Czech Republic has reached 72 years, a high figure among countries in central Europe. The infant mortality rate—the number of babies that die within a year of their birth—is 9 per every 1,000 live births. This is the lowest rate among the former Communist nations of Europe. But the country's birthrate continues to fall, and the rate of population growth has reached zero. In the future, this trend will force Czech workers to support an expanding population of aging retirees.

Language and Literature

The Czech language belongs to the Western Slavic family, a group that also includes Slovak and Polish. Czech speakers—especially those living in rural areas—have developed several local dialects. The Moravian dialect, for example, includes both Czech and Slovak expressions. Most members of ethnic minorities—including Germans and Poles—speak a second language in addition to Czech.

The Czech language actually has two forms. *Spisovna cestina*—the formal, written Czech—is used in the media and as a language of instruction at Czech universities. For everyday conversation, most people use *hovorova*, an informal Czech that is full of slang words and expressions. Unlike the written language, spoken Czech also includes some German and English words.

Czech literature dates to the early thirteenth century, when writers began recording legends, histories, and stories in the Czech language. In the 1400s, when the first Czech books were printed, the religious reformer Jan Hus published works of theology and important studies of Czech grammar and language.

When the German-speaking Habsburgs took over Bohemia and Moravia, their ban on Czech writing nearly destroyed the nation's literature. But in the late 1700s, the scholars Josef Dobrovsky and Josef Jungmann sparked a revival of Czech writing. They helped introduce the study of Czech in schools, where the Habsburgs had imposed German. During the 1830s, Jungmann compiled a new Czech dictionary that inspired poets and novelists to use the Czech language in their works.

Czech writers of this time penned narrative poems, folktales, and histories. Karl Macha, considered the finest Czech poet of his day, wrote *Maj*, a long poem about

Photo by BTE Bilde

A performance of Franz Kafka's *Metamorphosis* takes place in an urban park. Many theater companies hold open-air performances in Prague's parks and squares.

Photo by Czech News Agency

In his novels and stories, Kafta expressed the fear and isolation of people in the rapidly changing world of the twentieth century.

love and death. Other writers described the everyday lives and experiences of the Czech people. For example, Bozena Nemcova drew on Czech peasant life in her innovative novels and tales.

These literary themes changed in the early 1900s in the works of Franz Kafka, a German who lived in Prague. The characters in Kafka's novels and stories, which include *The Trial, Metamorphosis,* and *The Castle,* suffer fear and bewilderment in the face of modern civilization. Rainer Maria Rilke, another German writer from Prague, used complex symbols and imagery in his poetry.

Czechoslovakia's Communist regime tried to silence writers who expressed any criticism of the government or its policies. Many writers left the country, while others were imprisoned. Milan Kundera, Josef Skorecky, and Ivan Klima are skilled Czech writers who have won an international audience for their novels and stories. But only Klima stayed in Czechoslovakia for the duration of the Communist era.

Before the twentieth century, most Czech playwrights used patriotic themes and traditional Czech stories in their works. Under Communism, sarcastic comic plays gained a wide audience in underground theaters. Vaclav Havel, a famous playwright working in underground theater, spent several years in prison for mocking the regime.

Photo by Czech News Agency

The Czech writer Karel Capek wrote satirical plays that poked fun at modern science, industry, and politics. His play *R.U.R.,* written in 1921, was the first to use robots on the stage.

A small combo entertains on the Charles Bridge. Dozens of artists, musicians, and mimes perform for the crowds that gather on the historic span over the Vltava River.

Photo by Bernice K. Condit

Photo by Mansell Collection

Like many Czech composers, Antonin Dvorak drew on the folk music of Bohemia and Moravia in his works.

The Czech Republic has dozens of theaters that stage both modern and classical plays. Puppet theaters entertain young and old audiences, and many people consider Czech mimes to be among the best in the world. The famous Magic Lantern theater in Prague combines drama, mime, and special lighting effects.

Music

Czech music is closely tied to the country's traditional folksongs and instrumental pieces. Bedrich Smetana (1824–1884) wrote symphonies and operas using Bohemian folktales and legends. Smetana's work *Ma Vlast* (My Country) helped to inspire Czech nationalism in the late nineteenth century. Antonin Dvorak, the composer of *Moravian Duets* and *Slavonic Dances,* wrote his most famous symphony, entitled *From the New World*, in the United States. Dvorak also composed operas, choral music, string trios and quartets, and piano works.

The music and dialects of Moravia influenced Leos Janacek, who collected and arranged hundreds of Czech songs. Bohuslav Martinu, who studied and worked in France and the United States, was the most famous Czech composer of the mid-twentieth century.

Rock bands became a leading voice of political opposition during the 1980s, when several underground rock and jazz clubs opened in Prague. Czech cities still have large audiences for rock, jazz, and classical music. The Prague Spring Music Festival is one of Europe's biggest annual musical events. During this extravaganza, audiences crowd the capital's restored theaters and concert halls to enjoy opera, ballet, and symphonic music.

Food

Czechs enjoy a hearty cuisine known for its roast meats, wild game, vegetable dishes, dumplings, and pastries. Czech cooks have incorporated many dishes from neighboring countries over the years. Goulash, a meat stew spiced with paprika, arrived from Hungary. Sauerkraut (pickled cabbage) and roast goose came from Germany, and Austria contributed *schnitzel*, a breaded, seasoned veal cutlet. Sour cream, vinegar, and pickled vegetables from Slavic countries to the east add flavor and variety to Czech meals.

One of the most popular Czech meals includes roast pork, sauerkraut, and the widely popular *knedliky* (dumplings) that accompany many main dishes and soups. To make dumplings, Czech cooks boil or steam a mixture of flour, eggs, milk, and dried bread crumbs. Dumplings also may have fillings of plums or other fruit.

Independent Picture Service

Friends visit by candlelight in a wine cellar. These underground establishments—many of which offer music and other kinds of live entertainment—are especially popular in Moravia, an important wine-producing region of the country.

Appetizers include smoked meats, herring, sardines, or pickles, which come in all shapes, flavors, and seasonings. Roast goose or duck are favorite meats, and Czech chefs also prepare game meats such as hare and venison (deer meat). A meal of carp is traditional at Christmas.

For dessert Czechs enjoy pastries, fruit-filled pancakes, and cream or chocolate cakes. With their meals, adults sometimes drink beer—the best comes from the town of Plzen—or red wines from Moravia. *Slivovice,* or plum brandy, is a favorite after-dinner beverage.

Recreation and Sports

The forests, mountains, and lakes of Bohemia offer Czechs many opportunities for outdoor recreation. The country has downhill and cross-country skiing areas, and the mountains also draw rock climbers. Hikers can follow networks of marked trails in the Jesenik Mountains and in other highland regions.

Waterskiing and windsurfing are popular in the lakes of southern Bohemia, including Lipencka and Orlicka along the Vltava River. The rapids of the Vltava and Labe rivers, as well as smaller streams in

Photo © Massimo Sciacca

Vendors sell fresh fruit and vegetables at an open market. The new Czech government lifted the Communist regime's strict control of agriculture. This action has brought private farmers to the streets to sell their goods and has improved the supply of food.

Photo © Buddy Mays/Travel Stock

The rivers and streams of Bohemia offer water sports and other forms of recreation. Here, a fisherman trails a line for a catch from the Vltava River.

the mountains, challenge canoeists and kayakers.

Tennis has long been the favorite sport of young Czechs. Nearly every Czech town has tennis courts and organized clubs. The country has produced many international tennis champions, including Ivan Lendl, Hana Mandlikova, Martina Navratilova, and Jana Novotna. The Czechs are also enthusiastic soccer players. Thousands of adults and young people have joined local soccer teams. Other team sports—including ice hockey, volleyball, and basketball—draw large crowds of spectators.

Photo by Czech News Agency

Martina Navratilova, a Czech who emigrated to the United States in 1975, dominated the sport of women's tennis during the 1980s. Known throughout her career as an aggressive player with a strong serve, Navratilova retired in 1994.

Photo © Massimo Sciacca

Economic growth and foreign investment have allowed many Czech cities to restore streets, sidewalks, and buildings that have deteriorated during the twentieth century.

4) The Economy

The Czech Republic ranks as one of the most industrialized countries in Europe. The nation's large manufacturing sector dates from the eighteenth century, when Bohemia and Moravia made up the industrial heartland of the Habsburg Empire. The rich soils of Bohemia and Moravia also allow intensive farming, and the Czechs have mined coal and other minerals for centuries.

The Czech economy underwent a drastic change after World War II, when the new Communist government seized the nation's factories, farms, and mines. The government closely controlled the economy by setting prices, wages, and production levels. Through a series of five-year plans, Communist officials attempted to manage the supply of goods to meet demand. New factories were built in Plzen, Brno, and other cities, and the manufacturing sector employed a growing percentage of Czech workers.

But with their wages fixed, workers had little incentive to increase their production. When the supply of goods could not meet the growing demand, shortages developed. Czechs also experienced a lack of housing, fuel, and electricity. Poorly paid laborers rebelled against the system by not working at their jobs, causing further shortages. Strict laws against trade with non-Communist governments also hurt the Czechoslovak economy, which eventually ran out of money to invest in new equipment.

The revolution of 1989 ended central planning. The Czech Republic quickly

Photo © Massimo Sciacca

A crowded bakery serves rolls, croissants, loaves, and other tasty goods. Thousands of small private shops have replaced the state stores that supplied food and other consumer goods under Communism.

Independent Picture Service

A massive steel pipe rolls out of a cauldron at a Czech steel factory. Steelmaking thrived after World War II, when the Communist government saw heavy industries as the fastest way to achieve economic growth and a centralized economy.

Photo © Donna Carroll/Travel Stock

Like many craftspeople, this woman sells her homemade goods to the public from an outdoor table.

adopted a free market, in which supply and demand determine prices, wages, and production. The government began selling its state-operated industries and businesses to private companies, some of which are foreign firms. The German car company Volkswagen, for example, has bought Autoskoda, a Czech auto manufacturer.

By the mid-1990s, the government still had thousands of businesses left to sell. Obsolete companies that cannot compete in the new economy have closed, and many laborers are losing their jobs. In addition, the lifting of price controls has caused a sharp rise in the cost of living.

Photo © Buddy Mays/Travel Stock

A shop displays its wares along a sidewalk in the town of Ceske Budejovice.

Photo © Buddy Mays/Travel Stock

A tour boat cruises past small fishing craft on the Vltava River. With millions of travelers arriving each year to spend money on hotels, restaurants, and guided visits, Prague is benefiting from tourism.

Yet the transition to a market economy has succeeded in creating higher wages and better living standards for many workers. Gross national product (GNP)—the amount of goods and services produced by the country in a year—is slowly increasing. Trade with western Europe is on the rise, and tax breaks and other incentives have attracted thousands of foreign investors to the country.

Manufacturing

The busy Czech industrial sector dates to the years of Habsburg rule, when Bohemia provided the empire with munitions and

Photo by Doug Plummer

This chemical plant is typical of the manufacturers that have prospered in Bohemia and Moravia since the eighteenth century.

Independent Picture Service

Czechoslovakia's automobile industry supplied these Skodas to a limited market before the fall of Communism. By the mid-1990s, foreign companies were making new investments in Czech car factories, where workers earn less than laborers in western Europe.

weaponry. After World War II, the Communist government nationalized (took control of) most industries. But the country suffered a sharp decline in manufacturing in the 1960s. Factory managers had no authority to make decisions that could have improved the efficiency or productivity of their plants. In addition, because the nation did not trade or compete with western Europe, there was little need for modernization. By the mid-1980s, most industrial machinery in the Czech Republic was obsolete.

In the early 1990s, the new government sold thousands of state-owned enterprises

Independent Picture Service

For centuries, glassmaking has been an important industry among the Czechs. This modern glassworks in northern Bohemia draws on that long tradition.

Photo © Massimo Sciacca

Companies that make laundry soap have turned the side of this building into a gigantic billboard. Competition has prompted many Czech firms to advertise in the country's urban spaces.

to private firms. At first only Czech citizens could buy shares in the newly privatized companies. Later the government invited foreign companies to bid for ownership. The Czech Republic has also developed a stock exchange, through which the public can buy and sell company shares.

About 56 percent of the country's GNP now comes from manufacturing, which employs nearly one-third of the workforce. Food processing is the most important manufacturing activity. Other products include machinery, iron and steel, transportation equipment, chemicals, and petroleum.

The Czech Republic also has a healthy and growing light industry sector that produces beer, ceramics, clothing, paper, and textiles. Plzen is a major brewing center, and workshops in northern Bohemia have been making glass since the 1600s. Czech factories also turn out shoes, cigarettes, tires, radios, and newsprint.

Independent Picture Service

Piles of raw materials surround a busy steelworks.

Photo © John Kreul

Grain carts sit outside a storage building. Once forced to work on state-owned farms, many Czech farmers now operate their own estates free of government control.

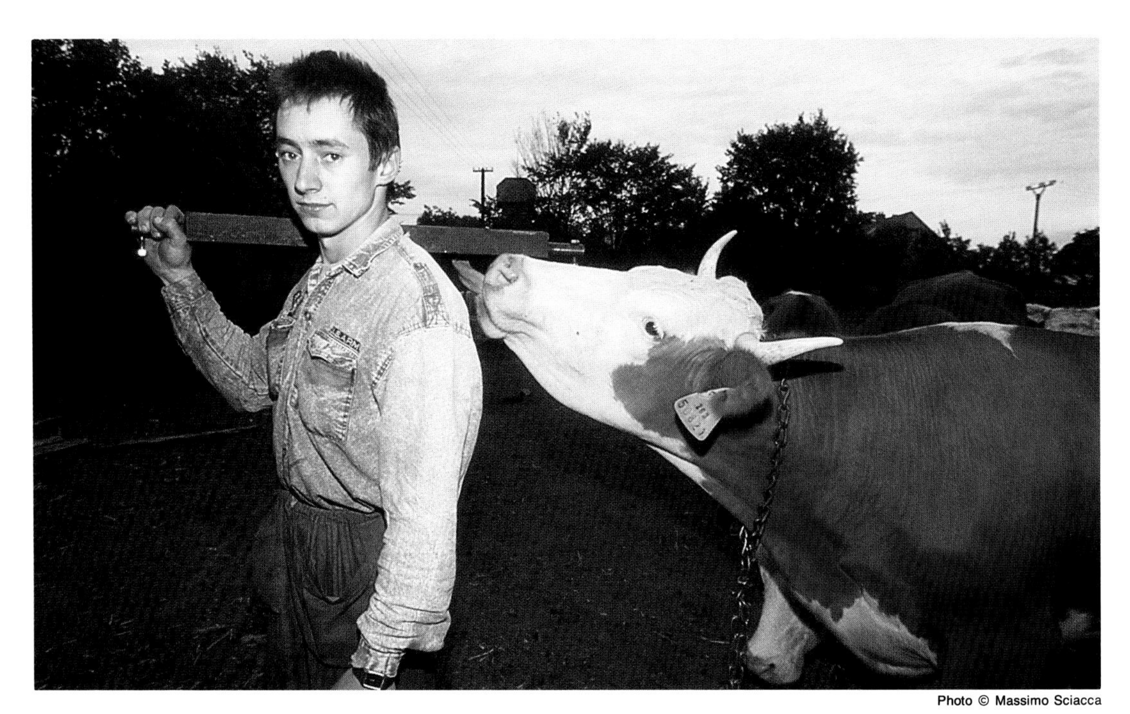

Photo © Massimo Sciacca

A young farmer brings a friendly cow out to pasture. Livestock makes up half of the Czech Republic's farm production.

Agriculture

After World War II, Czechoslovakia's agriculture, like its industries, came under state control. The government created more than 6,000 collective farms, where farmers shared their labor, equipment, and land. The government also set up large state farms—public acreages that paid fixed salaries to farmers.

The low pay on collective and state farms prompted thousands of young people to abandon farming and move to the cities, where they joined the better-paying manufacturing sector. This migration hurt agricultural production, and food gradually became scarce throughout the country.

State and collective farms still exist in the new Czech Republic, although the government is privatizing much of the country's farmland. The free-market economy, in which farmers can set prices for their goods, has ended shortages and has also improved the earnings of most Czech farmers.

The Czech Republic's most important crops are sugar beets, potatoes, wheat, and barley. Bohemia is one of the world's largest producers of hops, a main ingredient in beer. Livestock—hogs, sheep, cattle, and poultry—make up half of farm production, which in turn contributes 8 percent of the nation's GNP.

Energy and Mining

For many years, Czechoslovakia bought inexpensive electricity and fuel from the Soviet Union. As a member of the Soviet bloc, the nation was also able to import crude oil at low, controlled prices. Cheap fuel made Czechoslovakia dependent on Soviet energy imports and shielded the country from rises in the market price of oil.

Grain elevators tower over nearby fields in southern Bohemia. This region is one of the most intensely farmed areas of the Czech Republic.

Photo © Donna Carroll/Travel Stock

Independent Picture Service

The mines of Ostrava in Moravia produce coal and other minerals that factories and power plants use for energy and raw materials.

When the Soviet bloc collapsed, the Czech Republic suddenly had to pay much higher energy prices on an open market. At the same time, the growing economy increased the need for fuel and electricity to power factories. To meet demand, the Czech government adopted a conservation program and began construction of two nuclear power stations. By the mid-1990s, the Czech Republic was producing much more of its own energy at coal-burning and nuclear plants. Several hydroelectric facilities also supply electricity to homes and factories.

Mining employs about 3 percent of the workforce and plays a small but important role in the Czech economy. Coal deposits in Bohemia and northern Moravia offer a

Independent Picture Service

This control center in Ostrava monitors the distribution of electricity to homes and businesses in Moravia.

plentiful source of fuel for power plants. One of Europe's largest reserves of uranium ore lies in the Ore Mountains of northwestern Bohemia, where miners also extract antimony, magnesium, and mercury.

Foreign Trade

After World War II, Czechoslovakia's foreign commerce changed dramatically. Once an active and prosperous exporter, the nation began trading exclusively with its Warsaw Pact allies. Without competition from western Europe, Czech firms allowed their factories and products to grow obsolete. In the 1980s, the government introduced reforms to make Czech and Slovak companies more competitive, but the program failed to improve the quality of the nation's goods.

During the 1980s, Czechoslovakia ranked as one of the world's largest exporters of weapons. The Communist government supplied foreign nations and terrorist

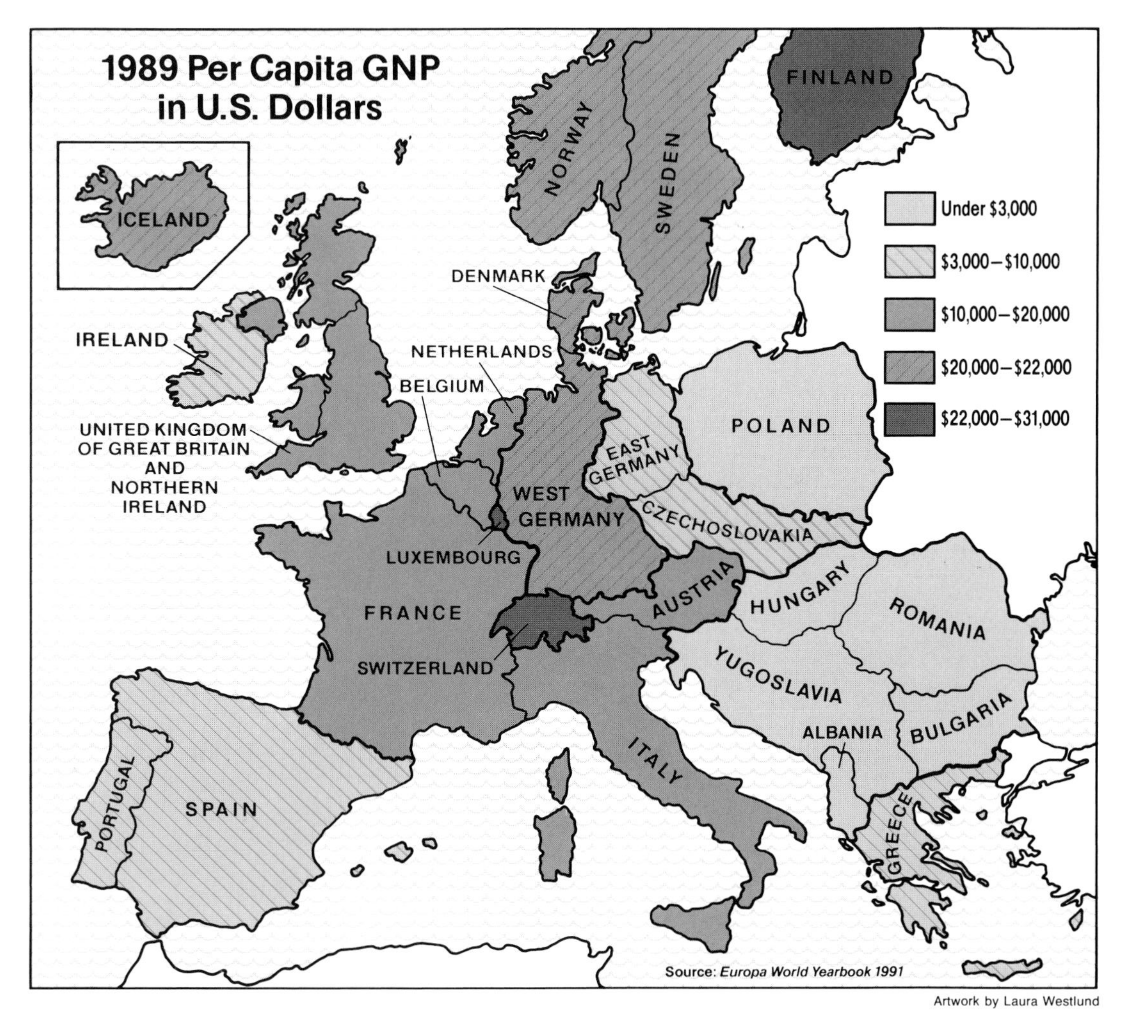

Artwork by Laura Westlund

This map compares the average wealth per person—calculated by gross national product (GNP) per capita—for 26 European countries in 1989. In that year, Czechoslovakia's figure was $5,820, making it one of the most productive of the Warsaw Pact nations. In 1993, after the division of the country, per-capita GNP in the Czech Republic was $3,077, while in Slovakia—where the economy declined for several years—the figure was $2,075.

A small stand offers crystal and glass objects for sale along a Bohemian roadside.

Photo © Donna Carroll/Travel Stock

organizations with high explosives and other items of destruction. Under international pressure to slow this trade, the Czech Republic stopped exporting weapons in the 1990s. To produce a wider range of products, the government is trying to attract foreign investors to retool weapons plants for other uses.

To increase its exports, the Czech government is building new trade alliances. The Czech Republic and Slovakia have formed a customs union, meaning the two nations will not tax goods exchanged between them. Poland, Hungary, the Czech Republic, and Slovakia have also set up a trading partnership known as the Visegrad Group.

At least half of all Czech exports now go to members of the European Union, a trade organization that the Czech Republic wishes to join. If the nation is admitted, it would be the first former Communist country with EU membership. This would greatly increase the market for Czech goods and could spur further foreign investment in the country.

Transportation and Tourism

The Czechoslovak Communist government improved the transportation system after World War II by building new railways, highways, and airports. The rail system was upgraded again in the 1980s to handle heavy industrial cargo. Freight and passenger trains each make up half the rail traffic.

By the 1990s, the Czechs had a well-developed system of highways and public transportation. Consumers are choosing from a wider range of private cars, and the government is planning to build new and better roadways. The nation is also improving its road links to other European countries. The national airline, CSA, provides direct flights to European and North American cities from Ruzyne airport near Prague.

Czechoslovakia was one of the first Communist European countries to open its borders to tourists. By the mid-1980s, as many as 40 million visitors a year were arriving. Tourism continued to thrive after the fall of Communism. Since the early 1990s, thousands of Czech citizens have

Photo © Massimo Sciacca

An electric tram carries commuters in Prague. Cars make slow progress on the city's narrow, winding streets, many of which have followed the same route for centuries.

Photo © Buddy Mays/Travel Stock

The majestic thirteenth-century Hluboka Castle rises near Ceske Budejovice.

Independent Picture Service

Blooming trees frame the castles and spires of Prague in the springtime.

set up shops, hotels, and other businesses that cater to foreign travelers.

Prague, where many historic streets and buildings have survived, remains the most popular destination in the country. Crowds of tourists visit Prague Castle, the Charles Bridge, the Powder Gate, and the famous clock tower in the Old Town neighborhood.

Outside of the capital, ancient castles dot the Bohemian countryside, and the artificial lakes along the Vltava River attract boaters and campers. Moravia is well known for its vineyards and wine cel-

Photo © Massimo Sciacca

Mirrors, pictures, and other goods crowd an antique shop. The nation's old homes provide a wealth of such items for modern decorators and collectors.

lars. East of Brno are the famous fields of Slavkov, where Napoleon defeated the Habsburg army in the Battle of Austerlitz.

The Future

Of all Europe's former Communist nations, the Czech Republic may have the best chance for prosperity and political stability. The country's peaceful transition to democracy and to a free-market system has improved foreign trade and production, and the growing economy is improving the nation's standard of living.

Independent Picture Service

A fisherman casts his line in the reflection of an old clock tower.

Photo © Massimo Sciacca

After their wedding, newlyweds lead their families on a small parade through their hometown.

Photo © Buddy Mays/Travel Stock

A Czech woman and her grandson wander along a narrow lane near the Moravian city of Brno.

But problems still exist. Unemployment is rising as state industries are privatized and modernized, creating less need for manual labor. The free market has also forced the country's citizens to pay higher prices for energy and food. In addition, inefficient energy use has damaged the nation's air, water, and soil. Many Czech cities suffer terrible pollution problems that must be solved before more foreign companies set up new facilities.

The transition from Communism will continue for many years, as the Czech Republic adjusts to an entirely new economic system. Nevertheless, the Czechs are eagerly embracing the changes and hoping to win a prominent place in a more united Europe of the future.

Photo by M. Bryan Ginsberg

Unusual sculptures and other artworks decorate the streets of some Czech cities.

Photo © Donna Carroll/Travel Stock

The Czech government has declared the entire city of Cesky Krumlov a national scenic monument.

Index